CW01500772

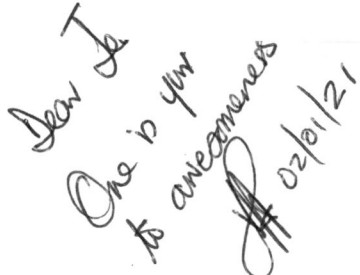

POWER OF

ONE

...the starting point of infinity

Richard Akita

Richard Akita

P.O. BOX CT11163,

Cantonments

Accra, Ghana

Alternatively, visit www.richardakita.com

Ordering Information:
Quantity sales. Special discounts are available on quantity purchases by corporations, churches, schools, associations and others. For details, contact the publisher at the address above, Email or call.

E-mail:
info@richardakita.com
Call: 0263 588 160

Printed by Launchpad Press
First Printing, 2015

ISBN: 978-9988-2-1122-6

Cover designed by Ryzard Akita of RA Productions

Editing and typesetting by Gird Center

www.girdcenter.org. 0263 144 621. Info@girdcenter.org

Dedication

This is for you, Najate, Marcelle and Ryzard. Thanks for always being my inspiration. And for all my clients who through my guidance continue to reap from the Power of One, may you never forget our mantra --- "Dare to Dream."

POWER OF ONE

Foreword

Really all of life boils down to one thing:

- One decision could change your life.
- One bad choice could change your life.
- One bold move could turn your business around.
- And one decision could determine whether you sleep in heaven or hell.

Every notable and successful person in history is known for ONE thing.

- Michael Jackson for music
- Michael Jordan for basketball
- Henry Ford for cars
- Steve Jobs for the apple brand
- Bill Clinton for politics

You must be decisive about the ONE thing you want the world to remember you for and this book provides you with the guidance for just that. Although action is particularly important to be successful, you cannot act without making a decision on what to do.

In Napoleon Hill's 'Think and Grow Rich,' he mentions that when he analyzed 700 people who were successful in accumulating a million dollars or more, he found that every single one had the habit of being decisive.

Decide today whether you want to be Significant or Mediocre. Decide what one thing you will do to head off in either direction.

Power of One should be a must read in all schools. Young people in particular must read this book next to their Bibles. Not only must you read Power of One, you also must determine and then act on your One!
God bless you, Richard, for giving young people a

practical guide to Significance".

Mr. Michael Ohene-Effah
Accra, 2015

POWER OF ONE

Introduction – One man

In the year 1870, a young man travelled to Fernando Po', an Island that is known today as Bioko in Equatorial Guinea. He returned to Ghana after about six years of stay on this island with nothing to show for except some cocoa pods.

Though the cocoa pods seemed insignificant to many people, Tetteh Quarshie held on to his cocoa seeds. As a new seed, a new idea, a fresh concept and perhaps something unique, it may not come as a surprise to you that he went through a series of challenges in trying to secure a piece of farmland to grow his rather amazing seeds. How could he convince people to believe in his idea, buy into his dream and support the journey of translating his vision into a tangible product? How could he, ONE man? Who would believe his report?

All the same, Tetteh Quarshie was consistent in following through with his passion. He planted the cocoa seeds into a forest. ONE man-hailing from Teshie in the southern part of Ghana found himself harvesting his produce from Akwapim-Mampong in the eastern belt of Ghana-ONE man.

Mr. Quarshie defied all odds. While people saw seeds he saw a harvest. Undeniably, with determination, failure will not overpower the flag of success. Although some people thought his idea will not work, he believed in his idea. ONE man.

Today in our country Ghana, his produce makes a significant contribution to the Gross Domestic Product. Cocoa remains the backbone of Ghana's economy. Farms, Roads and highways, tourist site and several other monuments have been named after him. ONE man. Parents who are not even related to Tetteh Quarshie name their children after him in his honour. ONE man. His story epitomizes how a single thought, decision or idea can translate into reality and grow to become the talk of nations or a house hold commodity. ONE man.

Your story is about to change---and you have to first understand that this book is a powerful missile which can revolutionize your thinking to cause a major launching pad in your life. With **Power of One**, I seek to challenge you, to value little beginnings, appreciate small things and follow through with your passion until it bears fruit.

Power Of One suggests to you that:

- You are ONE conversation away from your contract.
- You are ONE phone call away from your breakthrough.
- You have ONE more decision to make to seal that contract.
- You need to take ONE more step to achieve that goal.
- You have to push ONE more time to breakthrough that obstacle and to put a stop to that negative or abusive behaviour in your life.

It starts with ONE and the choice is yours. Fetch inspiration from the timeless stories I share in this book and distil the secret ingredients, the trusted potency, the power of compounding interest and the force in moving your ONE goal into becoming a reality. In *Power of One*, I present my thoughts to you on how you can identify that ONE thing that you can leverage for greatness. It is my suggestion that you journey through this book with a studious attitude, pondering over the quotes and Biblical references and make personal notes along the way.

There is a way to many and it begins with ONE.

Enjoy the read

Richard Akita

CONTENTS

.

One Idea

One Decision

One Action

1

WAKE UP TO YOUR ONE

"Small things are precursors of big things yet to come."

-Samuel Agyeman-Prempeh

Everybody can identify with the digit 'one.' One embodies diverse perspectives and as we discuss the subject of one and its features, you will come into a world of amazing discoveries. The word 'one' largely brings to mind an integer. It is essential however to see one not only as a numeral but also in addition to that as a phenomenon which comes with a myriad of powers.

Power of One does not only apply to mathematics but also essentially, it is power that applies to life at large.

One represents the starting point of anything. One is the foundation of every greatness ever attained. In the biological coitus of a man and woman, the potency of ONE is illustrated. During sex, there is a releases of millions of sperm cells into the uterus of the woman. In fact, researches reveal that a healthy adult male releases between 40 million and 1.2 billion sperms in a single ejaculation! The irony is, just ONE sperm meets a mature egg from the ovary for fertilization. ONE sperm. Approximately every month an egg will mature within one of the ovaries of a woman. ONE egg.

Is it possible that out of the numerous ideas you carry just ONE of them when acted upon and followed through with consistency can be your launchpad for achievement? Would you scale down your numerous ideas, pick ONE of them and pursue it consistently until success? Remember that out of the range of 40 million to 1.2 billion sperms released just one of them attains its mark.

The human brain is capable of producing thoughts between 12,000 and 50,000 in a single day, a research by the National Science Foundation (NSF) revealed. In fact, other findings peg the figure even higher to about 60,000. Could it be that out of the 60,000 ideas that flow through the region of your mind daily there is ONE that constantly compels you to pay it more attention than the others? Could that idea be the dynamo to break any rock in your life and lead you to your gold mine?

I submit to you this moment to pick that one idea, work consistently at achieving it, research more about it, work efficiently towards it and you will attain the mark of greatness. Would you dare act on your ONE now?

POWER OF ONE is not negligible in life. It is a force, dynamite, one is very important as a foundation to any end; a faulty or weak foundation leads to short lived advancement. If you are interested in seeing progress that is sustainable and lasting, then you have to pay attention to the foundation. ONE represents the foundation.

You may have countless ideas that compete for your attention and action, but perhaps the major breakthrough in your life will take place if you act on one of them. Indeed, ONE action nullifies the potency of a thousand great ideas.

One is not merely a starting point it is also a means to an end. Certainly, to keep your head above the waters during trying times there is the need for progress and ONE little step at a time can free you from the current discomfort. Consistency is important if we want to achieve development of any kind, ONE provides the means to the end we dream. Mathematically, the difference between two and one is one and the difference between three and two is one. This is to say, you can move from ONE to two by adding another ONE. In addition, to move from two to three, you will have to add ONE. Therefore, to achieve constant progress in business, ministry, academics or, career, you need to treat your new level as one, One-step at a time giving no room to complacency and indolence.

One is a hypothetical location or point in life, from where you make progress or gain advancement. In everything, you may find yourself doing in life, advance in one, and do not depart from it. Although ironic, ONE is indeed your starting point to infinity. It is pertinent therefore to view one as the available resources to work with and to develop. Numerically, one plus one is two. Would you find two the most comfortable or convenient spot? If your answer is NO, then treat two as a one. Thus, do not see your new situation as a destination, but rather point of transition to a higher position.

I am amazed to see people make little progress and then they are stuck at a point. Take the case of a young street hawker who by being diligent is able to source a corner in town where he placed a table to display his wares on. This young man can say that is a great leap, a jump from one to two. In due course, he moves on to acquire a shop. Now that is another giant step of progress. At this point, he increases his wares and his status changes. The question now is what does this new success mean to him? Has he arrived or is he still moving on by treating the current position as point one? This is the story of many people, they get relaxed and over excited at any new point in their lives, such that they make no effort to improve upon their lot or get better at what they do. Many businesses have gone into extinction simply because they fail to make improvements. ONE does not represent stagnation or stunted growth. ONE characterizes focus and development.

ONE idea

Your ability to translate your idea into a profit-making venture defines your business. All you need to start any business is just ONE idea. In this book, I bring into perspectives how Colonel Sanders, founder of Kentucky Fried Chicken, turned a garage kitchen business into a global business entity. The greatest asset to every business is its idea.

A negative situation may spark up a brilliant idea in you. Indeed, the wind of adversity causes the kite to soar high, as Napoleon Hill puts it. We have heard stories of people who own banks or savings and loans companies now, just because at some point in their lives, someone maltreated and humiliated them, as they wanted to secure loan facilities. There are accounts of some people who own airline companies due to travel frustrations and others who have started Human Resource firms because of dissatisfaction from previous encounters. They decided to write a new story from ONE idea.

ONE decision

Some people are motivated or driven to excellence by words that come their way. In some instances, you hear words that propel a quantum of greatness in you even when you are not the person to whom it addresses. The same way 'one idea', can spring from a bad experience, the word could also be a provocation or insult.

The diverse situations that can drive a person to achieve excellence are incredible. I mentioned earlier, how some individuals start their own companies out of frustration or humiliation suffered. The Virgin Airlines story is one such example. According to their website, thirty years ago, Richard Branson started Virgin Atlantic. However, what made him decide to go into the travel business in the first place?

As he reveals in a new film put together by HP Matter, it all came after being stuck in Puerto Rico while trying to get to the British Virgin Islands. "They didn't have enough passengers to warrant the flight, so they cancelled the flight," he explains. "I had a beautiful lady waiting for me in BVI and I hired a plane and borrowed a blackboard and as a joke I wrote Virgin Airlines on the top of the blackboard, $39 one way to BVI. I went out round all the passengers who had been bumped and I filled up my first plane."

After that, Richard decided that he was fed up with airlines that did not care about their passengers and he wanted to do something about it. A phone call to Boeing to find out if they had any 747s for sale and an airline was born.

ONE action

History records the story of a young man who was provoked into a fight with a man measuring over nine feet in height, a giant! The children of Israel were at war with the Philistines and David, the youngest of Jesse's sons went to bring his brothers food as he was instructed by Jesse (1 Sam. 17:17). When he arrived where his brethren were camped, he observed a giant who stood nine and a half feet tall.

His name was Goliath of Gath. He taunted the soldiers of Israel calling them cowards and just asked one man to come to him and fight him. The soldiers of Israel were scared because of his height. They just did not see how they could ever defeat him. David heard this giant insult the army of his God and was provoked into battle with him. The climax of the story is how young man; David could bring down the giant measuring over nine feet with just a single stone! Could you possibly be carrying in your hand a powerful tool that you probably have overlooked? Have you been thinking that idea cannot attract wealth? Permit me to put it to you that people are making money from the garbage.

Significance of One

2

THE STARTING POINT OF INFINITY

"If small is possible then big is only a step further."

-Samuel Agyeman-Prempeh

One is a very significant number among all integers; it is the first of counting numbers. One indicates the start of a thing; it marks inception and the starting point. One represents among other things unity, primacy, the first, and the best. It is independent of all other numbers and it is the source of all positive integers. Without one, there cannot be two, fourteen, two hundred and thirty-six and four thousand. In as much as this thought may seem basic, would you agree that all of these features of ONE emphasize the role of one in your life and in all that you do?

ONE is a reproductive force and a multiplier, inherent in it is the ability to reproduce to infinity. Therefore, if there is any height you may want to attain, a distance you desire to cover or depth you may want to get to, you would have to build on your ONE.

Every feat you may achieve in life, take off with A / (ONE) move, A decision, AN idea, and so on. Power Of One is an unavoidable and an essential ingredient of every success story here on earth. As the old adage goes, "a journey of thousand (1,000) miles begins with A (ONE) step." In like fashion, the journey to a multi-national firm, to a great ministry, to a prominent career, begins at a point, which may be an idea or decision. The most important thing is it starts on A/ (ONE) note. The truth is you do not need everything or all the things you need to be able to start. The simplest definition of big is small plus small plus small plus small to infinity. Thus big, is just an accumulation of small? Where small in this instance is one. Therefore, you have no reason or excuse legitimate enough to get you to remain at point zero. You are closer to one, than you are to hundred. It may interest you to know that, you can only get to hundred after attaining one. As a matter of principle, after holding on to one, you have to work towards the attainment of another one, which translates your position to two. Once you keep at that, you will get to your desired level of satisfaction and self-actualization.

In his best seller, Think and Grow Rich, Napoleon Hill tells a story of a treasure hidden in a piece of land. This information was revealed to a group of people. They dug several feet consistently but found nothing. Eventually they gave up. As the story continued, the group who finally discovered the treasure only had one more feet to dig! You are probably just a step away from winning that major contract. You are one foot away from your discovery. You cannot afford to give up now. One more step, one more try and bingo.

Threatened by a natural process of shoreline erosion, the Cape Hateras Light Station was moved INCH BY INCH, One-step at a time, 2900km intact from its original position to a new location. Your dream will not die, if you will study a little more, research an hour extra, rehearse just one more time, you would erupt a standing ovation. Get up there. ONE more to go, ONE more, you can do it. It is possible. Challenge yourself. Amaze your critics. See your dreams transpose before your very eyes. Just ONE more try.

There is a word that fascinates me so much, 'schmooze'; it refers to an informal conversation, a casually conversation held in a friendly way. These days many young entrepreneurs schmooze their way into business. Les Brown once said, 'your network determines your net worth. There is probably ONE key person you have to meet to make your dream a reality. Among all the women, you need to meet the ONE to be your spouse. At that reception, the man you offered a seat to, or sat by or rather walked towards and offered a firm grip handshake or a priceless smile could be that ONE investor you have been praying for. You are ONE person away from your goal. Do not miss……. the ONE.

"This is how business work: A knows B, B knows X, the answer is in 'who knows Z?"

-Samuel Agyeman-Prempeh

The bible in Zechariah 4:10, admonishes us to regard and attack importance to small beginnings (ONE). Some people tend to regard their starting points as worthless and impotent. I would like to suggest to you that you treat your "ONE" with all seriousness, for inside it is the seed of greatness. If you carry your ONE idea in your heart, you will attract all the resources needed to accomplish it.

Bryce Courtenay also says, "When men can be made to believe, then they can be made to win." In other words, the man who is able to generate an idea and hold on to it is the man who would be able to handle the aftermath of that idea. Yet, it all starts with ONE, from a point, on a day. Heights attained on ONE are sustainable heights.

The Piccolo

The Piccolo is an instrument in the flute family, a rather small instrument that most likely gained its name from 'piccolo' the Italian word for 'small'.

Despite how small the piccolo is; it plays a significant function in orchestra. In an orchestra, there are several bigger instruments from the string family; for example, the violin and cello, the Brass Family; like the trumpet, trombone and the percussion family like the xylophone and bass drums.

Despite the sizes of other instruments, in reality the sound the piccolo produces are often ONE octave higher than when it is written (in musical theory). As such the piccolo player is designated, a particular position called the 'assistant principal' to play along the rather big instruments such as the violin. Why? Well, the Piccolo adds sparkle and brilliance to the overall music due to the ONE-octave transposition higher.

Is your idea the one-octave idea being searched for?

FOCUS

3

FOLLOW ONE COURSE UNTIL SUCCESS

"The successful man is the average man focused."

-   *Anonymous*

The words focus and diligence are used interchangeably in most literature. Diligence is being dedicated to one's path. There are millions of doctors in the world, but if you are to randomly mention the names of doctors. Our list will be incomplete without the likes of Professor Frimpong Boateng and Prof. Badu Akosa both from Ghana. If you are to mention the names of lawyers, you are sure to mention names like Phillip Addison, Tsatsu Tsikata and others. In the field of entrepreneurship too, prominent names include Prince Kofi Amoabeng, Kwame Despite, Joseph Siaw Agyepong and many others. The same applies to all other professions. The key thing that makes the above men stand out is diligence and their focus on what they have been called into.

Diligence is staying focused on your assignment; facing ONE thing to the end. A well-known definition of the word focus renders it 'acronymically' as *Follow One Course Until Success*. Thus, after you follow ONE course or path to the end, success will be an encounter for you. The difference between ordinary and extraordinary men is 'extra' and you attain that extra through diligence and ability to follow ONE path to the end.

Men without 'focus are like 'locusts', one man of God said. Locusts jump from one place to another seeking a place of comfort; neglecting the fact that they can transform their current standing, which is their ONE into a more profitable venture. Henry Ford once said, "I think nothing of a man who was wiser yesterday, than he is today." I believe such a man lacks diligence in his field of endeavour. Diligence causes one to get closer to excellence, and diligence actually comes with striving for excellence. Be diligent at what you do and that will propel you to improve in your life.

There is a call for you to stay focused in every area of life you find yourself; this calls for adequate planning, before pushing towards the achievement of a goal. As a student, you need to employ this principle of life in your academics. This principle of life is also applicable in your business, career and ministry. Focus is an infallible, potent and result-yielding phenomenon of life.

The ability to stay focused and diligent causes an individual to stand out among his contemporaries.

"Do you see a man (who) excel in his work? He will stand before kings; He will not stand before unknown (men)"

-Proverbs 22:29

We have successful young entrepreneurs like Derrydean Dadzie (Dream Oval) and Papa Kwame Osei (Pkog), whose names are mentioned as giants in their industries. This is because; they were diligent with the little they started with and made the best out of it. This reiterates in a Ghanaian adage, "The child who knows how to wash his hand eats with elders." All you need to transform yourself or your business into a twenty-year-old asset when it is only a year old, is to stay focused on what you have in hand.

God Almighty, the God of orderliness, rewards diligence and ability to stay focused. In Deuteronomy 28:1, "Now it shall come to pass, if you diligently obey the voice of the LORD your God, to observe carefully all His commandments which I command you today, that the LORD your God will set you high above all nations of the earth."

Wow, what a reward! Isaac, the father of irrigation farming, obeyed the voice of the Lord and remained where God asked him to be and became a great man.

What about these men too, Benjamin Franklin, Michael Faraday, Albert Einstein, Walt Disney and J. D. Rockefeller, whose names have been engraved in and on our memories? Their names can never be erased from our books of history.

Do you really want to make a mark and a difference in your life, academics, business, ministry or career? There is the need for purpose of action and location if you want to attain your desired goal. I challenge you to add diligence to your virtues. Let us examine the life of Jesus Christ. He had a very successful ministry and accomplished his purpose on earth in a space of 33 years. Is that not just a remarkable feat? Some ministries and businesses have been in existence for over five decades, and yet cannot find their place. Some folks have wasted their youth and their old age on pursuing things that do not matter to life. Quoting Jesus Christ in John 18:37, He made clear His reason for existence on earth. He came into this world to achieve a particular purpose---just ONE.

"For this (one) course, came I into the world."
-John 18-37. (Emphasis added)

There is just ONE purpose for His coming into this world. Could this be the secret to Jesus' ever flourishing and growing ministry while on earth? His legacy continually lives with us, just look at the multitude that has turned to the kingdom, because of a simple act of FOCUS.

Staying focused makes a person, a business, a ministry lives on after its existence.

On this note, permit me to suggest to you to be in constant search of your purpose. Your purpose defines you. As an individual, you have been engineered to achieve your purpose. As you focus on achieving your purpose, all other things will aggregate towards you. It is unfortunate that only a few people spend time in prayer, word study, introspection and research to identify their purpose. I challenge you today to find out that ONE thing that defines you. That ONE thing you are made to do. Napoleon Hill calls it Definite Chief Aim, Mike Murdock refers to it as Assignment and Dr. Myles Munroe passionately calls it Purpose. There is a definite chief aim for which you were created. You are on a specific assignment. Your greatest victory on earth will be rooted in your purpose. I challenge you to live a purpose driven life.

Nothing ever becomes dynamic, until it first becomes specific. I call that focus. The price of lack of focus is very unbearable; it is more expensive than staying focused. A shift in focus, can lead to the collapse of a whole business empire, or even lead to misery in a man's life. People who seek after others do not end up with results.

"Troubles multiply for those who chase after gods......"

-Psalm 16:4 NLT

One great mind said: The pain of discipline weighs in gram, the pain of regret weights in kilograms.

"Purpose your dreams with a tenacious attitude for surely the reward always outweigh the pain."

-Richard Akita.

What do you think of the quotes you just read? The message here is that those who cannot stay focused shall receive more problems than they already have. On the other hand, the benefits that accrue from diligence and focus are just amazing. In business you take calculated risks; you do not jump after every business that comes your way. I urge you to STAY FOCUSED.

One of the greatest enemies to your glorious destiny is distraction. Distractions are side attractions seeking your attention to prevent you from reaching your destination. Distractions sway you off your object of focus. Just like using a camera, you need to focus on the object you want to capture. This means to achieve the best and the finest you need to focus. When you focus on the little you have or on your starting point, it makes you a Centre of attraction, which commands attention in your favour to cause you to scale heights.

"The greatest deterrent to racism and gender imbalance is excellence," Oprah Winfrey once said. Thus, when you have excellence to show, nobody cares about your race or your gender.   Focus and commitment breed excellence. A person without results receives insults. To avoid the insults of society, there is a dire need to produce results; which is unachievable without focus.

There is a clarion call to and for diligence and focus, to the youth as currently. The baton is in their hands, to move nations and continents to their desired post. In Peter's epistle, he said, "therefore, brethren, be even more diligent to make your call and election sure, for if you do these things you will never stumble." - 2 Peter 2:10. Thus, you are in this country and continent for a time as this, and if you put on the garment of diligence you shall never fail at what you set your heart on to achieve. Locate the "ONE" and stay focused on it. In due course, you shall see the beauty of your end.

"Most people have no idea of the giant capacity we can immediately command when we focus all of our resources on mastering a single area of our lives."

-Tony Robbins

One Lesson Stories

4

Be The One Story You Want To Tell

Greatness is not measured by what a man or woman accomplishes, but by the opposition he or she has overcome to reach his goals.

- ***Dorothy Height***

The story of the chicken Bucket

Colonel Sanders established KFC several decades ago, but today it is a worldwide business. How did he start? His is a very amazing success story. David Harland Sanders was a sixth-grade dropout, a farmhand, an army mule-tender, a locomotive fire fighter, a railroad worker, an aspiring lawyer, an insurance sales clerk, a ferryboat entrepreneur, a tyre sales clerk, an amateur obstetrician, an unsuccessful political candidate, and several other things he engaged in to make ends meet for himself. At the age of 65, a misfortune befell him such that all he had was a social security check and a secret recipe of fried chicken, which he learnt from his mother at a young age. In 1930, Colonel Sanders started cooking for hungry travellers at a gas service station in Corbin, Kentucky. He soon introduced what he called "home meal replacement," selling complete meals to busy strapped families. As more people started coming strictly for the food, he moved across the street to increase his capacity. Over the next decade, he perfected his secret blend of 11 herbs and spices and the basic cooking technique that is still in use today.

In 1955, confident of the quality of his fried chicken, the Colonel devoted himself to developing his chicken franchising business. Less than 10 years later, Sanders had more than 600 KFC franchises in the U.S. and Canada.

Kentucky Fried Chicken, pioneered by Colonel Harland Sanders, has grown to become one of the largest quick service food service systems in the world – with more than a billion "finger lickin' good" Kentucky Fried Chicken dinners served annually in more than 80 countries and territories.

I believe you followed the story closely, the colonel started at point ONE (a social security check and secret recipe for fried chicken). This was the starting point and foundation of Kentucky Fried Chicken. He worked on what was available as his ONE by cooking for hungry travellers at a gas service station. After some years, he made progress to another location and perfected the herbs he used for spicing the chicken and the basic cooking technique he used. You realize that, at a very new point he made progress and was never relaxed or satisfied. Today, he has franchisees all over the world. Isn't this success for one who started at a retirement age?

The secret behind this great success story is ONE idea of spicing chicken. Every idea starts funny, so do not be bothered about how crazy your idea sounds. Keep working on it and you will see it become the next big thing for the world to see.

J.K. Rowling

J.K. Rowling is a British novelist and a multiple award winner for her books. The most famous of her books is the Harry Porter series. These books have gained worldwide attention, won multiple awards, and sold more than 400 million copies, and been the basis for a chain of films which have become the highest-growing film series in history. The author saw her life transform from living on state benefits to a multi-millionaire status in a space of 5 years. Do not doubt it yet, the secret shall be unveiled soon.

J.K. Rowling hit her rock of gold with the Harry Porter series. She conceived the idea on a delayed train from Manchester to London in 1990. She conceived just an idea, and it became a novel and now a series with seven sequels. Today, she is the United Kingdom's bestselling living author, with sales in excess of 238 million pounds. Her fortune is estimated at 560 million pounds, according to 2008 article by Sunday Time Rich list. This makes her the twelfth richest woman in the United Kingdom. Forbes ranked her as the forty-eighth most powerful celebrity in 2007, and the most influential woman in Britain in 2010. All of these laurels and accolades by reason of just ONE series, Harry Porter series. Note that she has other books in addition to Harry Porter series. She is the author of 'The Casual Vacancy' and 'Fantastic Beast' and 'Where to find them'. Yet it started with ONE book. That is how it works.

Today, Rowling is a brand in literature. Her story emphasizes the truth that, ONE is a step into infinity.

In her commencement speech, The Fringe Benefits of Failure, and the Importance of Imagination, delivered at the Harvard University, she said,

"So why do I talk about the benefits of failure? Simply because failure meant a stripping away of the inessential,

I stopped pretending to myself that I was anything other than what I was, and began to direct all my energy into finishing the only work that mattered to me. Had I really succeeded at anything else, I might never have found the determination to succeed in the one arena I believed I truly belonged. I was set free, because my greatest fear had been realized, and I was still alive, and I still had a daughter whom I adored, and I had an old typewriter and a big idea.

And so rock bottom became the solid foundation on which I rebuilt my life. You might never fail on the scale I did, but some failure in life is inevitable. It is impossible to live without failing at something, unless you live so cautiously that you might as well not have lived at all – in which case, you fail by default."

My dear friend, I urge you keep focus on your ONE, and you will experience a major turnaround just like J. K. Rowling. If ONE could amount to millions and change someone's status in 5 years, you can also have a similar feat in business, career and ministry.

Grandma Moses

Grandma Moses (Anna Mary Robertson Moses) was a renowned American folk artist. She began painting at the age of 78. She is a great example of an individual who successfully began her career in the arts at an advanced age. Her story is one that exhibits the power of ONE.

At an early age of 12, when she was live-in housekeeper, she expressed appreciation for the paints of the families she worked for. One of the families that she worked for, noticing her love for, and interest in their paints, purchased for her chalk and wax crayons so that she could start her own artwork. At a young age, she made pictures out of yarn. At an early age of 20, in marriage, she enjoyed doing needlework such as sewing and embroidery. With needle and thread she would do make pictures on fabric. At late 78, she decided to take up painting seriously. Her art is classified as folk art, which is self-taught.

She viewed her art as something she enjoyed doing, and it provided some extra money. Her artworks were paid for at very high prices. At age 80, a painting, which was first sold for $5, was sold between $8,000 and $10,000. Isn't this amazing? Presidents honoured her, several books have been written about her. A "Grandma Moses Day" was proclaimed in New York.

Someone made millions of dollars out of hobby, which she took serious at a late age of 78 years. The question now is what would have been the story if she started earlier? Perhaps she could have been a Bill Gates or an Oprah Winfrey. The truth, however, is that age is not a factor or an inhibitor to greatness, if you have your eyes set on ONE thing.

Another remarkable thing to note about Grandma Moses story is how she held on to her passion with consistency from the age 12 and followed through with her ONE throughout the years. You may be wondering why she took so long to take a firm decision to show the world her art. For me, she was perfecting her art and when she was ready to show her work, she absolutely shone brighter than the world had ever seen of a 78-year-old. She did not have any form of formal education in pursuit of a career in art. Many people give up too early on their dreams and aspirations, and they end up wandering from place to place without settling on a particular thing that they can describe their life with.

The Bible calls attention to not giving up in Habakkuk 2:3, "For the vision (is) yet for an appointed time; But at the end it will speak, and it will not lie. Though it tarries, wait for it; because it will surely come, it will not tarry." There is always an appointed time, and your dream shall surely come to fruition if you follow through with consistency. It may take a long while for you to see the benefits of your hard work and passion but there comes the day where the rewards are as clear as the light of the day. Just keep working towards that day.

Grandma Moses followed her passion consistently; today her name comes up as one of the giants in the Arts. At one point in her painting career, she accumulated a sale worth more than the aggregate of sales she made for all her year on the farm. The question is, how differently would her life have been had she focused on painting her entire life?

It Is Possible!

These Seven Christian entrepreneurs have seen their businesses expand globally and become household names:

John D Rockefeller

Rockefeller was the founder of the Standard Oil Company, which dominated the oil industry period. He revolutionized the petroleum industry and set the standard for modern philanthropy.

He was a devout Christian who taught in Sunday school and supported many church-based projects throughout his life. Rockefeller was quoted as saying "God gave me money," and he did not apologise for it. He followed John Wesley's principle of "gain all you can, save all you can, and give all you can."

From his very first pay cheque, Rockefeller tithed ten percent of his earnings to his church. As Rockefeller's wealth grew, his giving also increased, with most of his giving going towards educational and public health causes, as well as basic science and the art.

He became the world's richest man and the first American worth more than a billion dollars. After taking into account inflation, he is often regarded as being the richest person in modern history.

Tyler Perry

Tyler Perry went from being homeless to selling out theatres within a few years. He is an outspoken Christian who credits his success to God. In 2006, he established Tyler Perry Studios and in 2008, it moved to its current location - a 200,000 square foot studio facility situated in Southwest Atlanta, USA. In 2013, Forbes estimated his earning at US$78 million.

Henry Heinz

Henry Heinz was a nineteenth century Christian businessman who founded the Heinz Company in 1969. Heinz based his business on Christian principles and proclaimed that his success was a direct result of his faith in God. Heinz was committed to bringing out the best in people and his company was credited for its fair treatment of workers and for pioneering safe and clean food preparation. Today the Heinz Company is worth around $12 billion. Its most famous product is tomato ketchup, with 650 million bottles of Ketchup sold every year.

Cher Wang

Cher Wang is a Taiwanese entrepreneur who co-founded smart phone maker, HTC Corporation and VIA Technologies. Her late father was Wang Yung- Ching, who was one of the richest individuals in Taiwan. Wang is a devout Christian who was quoted as saying that the Bible is "the best book about management practice." One of the most important things she has learned from the Bible is that a person must have a vision otherwise; he or she will be destroyed. The vision for HTC Corporation came during her early career. Wang was at that time working with First International Computer. As she dragged bulky, heavy computers to client offices, she knew there must be a better way of designing a computer that could fit in the palm of your hand. In 1997, she acted on that vision and HTC Corporation was born.

In May 2011, Forbes ranged her and her husband Wen Chi Chen as the richest people in Taiwan. Following some challenges with HTC's sales dropping in recent months, Forbes ranked her husband's as Taiwan's 13th richest people with a combined net worth of US$2.5 billion in 2013.

Sam Walton

Sam Walton was an American businessman and entrepreneur, best known for founding the Wal-Mart retail stores. With his strong Christian background based on ethics and hard work, Walton excelled in school, college, and business. Early in his career, he worked as a management trainee for J.C. Penney.

In 1998, Walton was included in Time's list of 100 most influential people of the 20th Century and Forbes ranked him as the richest man in the United States from 1982 to 1988. Interestingly, Bill Gates only topped the list for the first time in 1992, the year Walton died.

Strive Masiyiwa

Strive Masiyiwa is a Zimbabwean born businessman who founded Econet Wireless is now a global telecommunications group with operations, investments and offices in more than 15 countries. A born-again Christian, Strive Masiyiwa was quoted as saying that he reads his bible for at least 4 hours a day – if he is busy! He tithes 10% of his annual income to his Church. Together with his wife, he personally pays the school fees for over 22,000 Zimbabwean orphans. According to Forbes, as of November 2013, he has an estimated net worth of US$600million.

Mary Kay Ash

Mary Kay Ash retired in 1963 after she was passed over for a promotion in favour of a man that she had trained. She intended to write a book to help women in business. The book soon turned into a business plan, and in 1963, Mary Kay Ash began Mary Kay Cosmetics with a $5,000 investment.

The founding principle of Mary Kay Cosmetics was known as the "Golden Rule," upon which the company's marketing plan was developed to allow women to advance by helping others to succeed. She advocated "praising people to success" and her slogan "God first, family second, career third" expressed her belief that the women in her company should keep their lives in the right balance.

Mary Kay was honoured as the number 1 leading female entrepreneur in American history.

Reference:
http:www.mykingdombusiness.com/7-inspirational-Christian-entrepreneurs/

Personal Action Plan: A Plan for ONE

"There is nothing ordinary about you. You are endowed with unlimited creative potential, so be the solution in your sphere of influence."

-Richard Akita

"You can have brilliant ideas but if you cannot get them across your ideas won't get you anywhere."

-Lee Lacoca

In reading the amazing stories of how people have impacted history by harnessing their dominant potential, I will not be surprised if you have been stirred up to look into yourself and discover that ONE thing you can leverage for greatness.

At this point, I will employ you to get a pen or pencil and turn to page 33 for an exercise after reading the following passages:

Inner Search

Start with the process of introspection. Be sincere and objective in identifying behavioural patterns that you may call positive. Also, consider how these behaviours have affected your life. As you do this, observe habits that have a negative impact on you. Take note of how these positive and negative tendencies have affected your life. What lessons can you draw from these behavioural patterns to help you achieve your vision? Which goals, dreams or aspirations do you intend to achieve? My suggestion is that you settle on ONE. Which of your goals are you most passionate about? Which of them excites you the most?

My suggestion once again is, settle on ONE. Most often in your quest to achieve that ONE goal, most of the other goals would be achieved.

"If you do not express your own original ideas, if you do not listen to your own being, you will have betrayed yourself." -Rollo May

Mission

Here again the subject of Purpose is key. This time let us talk of your mission. Your mission is a specific assignment for which you have been created. There is a specific calling on your life. There is a specific role to play. Everything else falls in place in the achievement of this assignment. Do not relish being a jack-of-all trades. You have been called unto ONE major assignment. Your quest here is to pray to find out the distinct mission for which you are to accomplish.

"I begin with an idea then it becomes something else."

-Pablo Picasso

Now a (ONE) river went out of Eden to water the garden, and from there it parted and became four riverheads.

-Genesis 2:10

Routine

Here the focus is on the power of consistency, developing powerful habits that can help you to achieve your goals. What small changes or innovations can you bring into your daily, weekly or monthly routine to help you towards achieving your goals? Establish a routine towards the achievement of your goals. The Webster Dictionary explains the word routine as a regular way of doing things in a particular order. Researchers have revealed that it takes about twenty-one (21) to thirty (30) days for habits to develop. Distinct opinions may exist on the subject of how habits are formed however most pivot on the fact that it is a result of repletion.

"We are what we repeatedly do. Excellence then, is not an act but a habit."

-Aristotle

"Success is not something you do once; it is something you do repeatedly."

-Dr. Mensa Otabil

I would suggest you flip back to reflect on these quotes again, later. Now let us look at some seven routine activities that can help you develop your ONE.

Record

Any time, you have a thought that requires an action, record that thought. Write it down or speak it into an audio recording device.

Be Prepared always

In order to record your thoughts, you will need to keep writing materials or a voice recorded with you at all places. You may keep them in your bedside cabinet, bathroom, or in your car.

Do It

Decide the next action for every task. Once you do this, you have three options and ONE decision to make. You do it, delegate it or defer it. May I suggest an idea to you? **DO IT**.

Review

On a weekly basis, conduct a review of your diary and task list. Look for patterns of success and frustration. For example, who are the people that deserve most of your time? Where are you actually spending your time? If there is a gap between these two answers, which most likely would occur, realign your dairy and task list quickly and decisively.

Limit Decision Fatigue

Limit decision fatigue, which is proven to diminish the quality of your decisions later in the day.

Prioritize

Prioritize all of the following: exercise, meditation, visualization, learning and gratitude.

Conclusion

5

THE NEW YEAR RESOLUATIONS - CAN YOU

REDUCE THEM TO ONE?

"But seek first the kingdom of God and His
righteousness, and all these things shall be added to
you." Matthew 6:33

As a critical observer and a deep thinker, I make a lot of analysis and observations. One of the key observations is what propelled me to put this book, **Power of One,** together. My observation revealed to me how people struggle in achieving their goals and visions for their life. I came to realize that many people decide to do so many things at a time. The long lists individuals make as their resolution pledge when a new year is approaching, probably confirms my observation. The frustrations only increase as people are unable to attain the mark for which they set themselves. Most people often set many and arguably unpractical goals.

What I have deduced is that, many of the things we want to achieve are often rooted in ONE major vision. Many of the habits you want to break are probably rooted in a particular addiction, lifestyle or pattern of behaviour. Thus, we need to pay attention to this ONE thing, a key pivot in regulating the other areas of our lives.

I am convinced that taking time to study Power Of One has provided you the opportunity to search and identify your purpose, prioritize your goals and settle on the achievement of ONE major vision, with the understanding that all the other things will gravitate towards it.

As a firm believer of the Gospel, there is ONE goal that we should all align ourselves towards. The Bible tells us to seek ONE thing; The Kingdom of God and His righteousness; and all other things will be added unto us. This is where my message has been rooted. That if we, primarily, seek other things, we are likely to miss them and as such miss the major thing as well, 'The Kingdom of God, and His righteousness.' On the other hand, if we focus on the ONE thing that is needful, the ONE thing that is important, like focusing on the Kingdom of God and His righteousness, we are presented with other blessings.

"The Power of One is above all things the power to believe in yourself, often well beyond any latent ability you may have previously demonstrated. The mind is the athlete, the body is simply the means it uses to run faster or longer, jump higher, shoot straighter, kick better, swim harder, hit further, or box better."

-Bryce Courtenay, The Power Of One

"I fear not the man who has practiced 10,000 kicks once, but I fear the man who practiced one kick 10,000 times."

-Bruce Lee

A PLAN FOR ONE

Inner Search

Which of your habits and behavioural patterns do you identify as positive?

_____

_____

_____

_____

_____

_____

_____

_____

_____

_____

Which of your habits and behavioural patterns do you identify as negative?

_____

_____

_____

_____

_____

_____

_____

_____

_____

_____

_____

_____

What lesson can you learn from these patterns to help you achieve your vision?

_____

_____

_____

_____

_____

_____

_____

_____

_____

_____

_____

_____

Which goals, dreams or aspirations do you intend to achieve?

_____

_____

_____

_____

_____

_____

_____

_____

_____

_____

_____

_____

_____

Which of your goals are you most passionate about?

Mission

Write down your mission after you have prayed and searched within yourself.

_____

_____

_____

_____

_____

_____

_____

_____

_____

_____

_____

Routine

What small changes or innovations can bring into your daily, weekly or monthly routine to help you achieve your goals?

_____

_____

_____

_____

_____

_____

_____

_____

_____

_____

ABOUT THE AUTHOR

Richard Akita is a Life Performance Coach and Entrepreneur. He draws his inspiration from past encounters and has an insatiable desire to learn from every opportunity whether positive or negative. As a life performance coach and leadership developer, he has dedicated his life work and passion to empowering others to pursue their dreams.

Richard is passionate to see people serve their community with excellence and maximize the use of their gifts and talents. He enjoys the opportunities of working alongside clients as they achieve their goals. His practical teaching style coupled with motivational skills encourages his clients to discover and utilize their greatest assets in worship and service to God and their community.

He is involved in different leadership positions in ministry and manages successful businesses. With over 25 years of experience in key management positions within the retail, cleaning and real estate industries, he has and continues to acquire a wealth of knowledge in the business arena, which he shares with his clients equipping them to excel.

Richard Akita has two books to his credit; Power of One………. The starting point of infinity and Every Day in Love, Inspirational love expressions & insightful quotes.